Alfred's Basic Piano Library

Piano
Composition Book
Level 2

AF270822

This COMPOSITION BOOK is designed to be used with *Alfred's Basic Piano Library*, LESSON BOOK 2. The book is coordinated page-by-page with the LESSON BOOK, and assignments are ideally made according to the instructions in the upper right corner of each page of the COMPOSITION BOOK.

This Composition Book reinforces concepts as they are presented in the Lesson Book, and specifically focuses on the development of creativity and compositional skills. In the beginning, students may need help notating their pieces correctly. Eventually students should be able to complete the assignments at home if the instructions for each exercise are reviewed at the lesson. Ask students to play directly from the music they have composed so they can see the correlation between what they have written and how the music actually sounds. This reinforces new concepts and strengthens reading skills.

It is possible to use this book even after a student has progressed to higher levels. This can solidify concepts already learned and can stimulate and develop creativity and compositional skills. The book can also be used with students in other methods.

Encourage students to use the limitations given in the book as a guide, but allow them to explore beyond those limitations. This will develop their natural curiosity and creativity.

Examples for the teacher are given on page 32.

Valerie Cisler • Deanna Walker-Tipps

Dotted Quarter Notes

A **DOTTED QUARTER NOTE** is equal to a quarter note
tied to an eighth note.

In $\frac{2}{4}$, $\frac{3}{4}$ or $\frac{4}{4}$ time, the **DOTTED QUARTER NOTE** is
almost always followed by an **EIGHTH NOTE** (♩. ♪)!

1. The counting is given at the beginning of each *Clap Rap*.
   Complete the counting, writing **1 & 2 & 3 & 4 &** in $\frac{4}{4}$ and **1 & 2 &** in $\frac{2}{4}$
2. Clap and say the words to each *Clap Rap* with your teacher.
3. Using ♩ ♩. ♩ ♫ and ♪ write the matching rhythm on the lines below the words.
4. Using the hand positions indicated, improvise a melody that matches the rhythm of each *Clap Rap*. When you **IMPROVISE,** you **EXPERIMENT** with sound.

Clap Rap No. 1

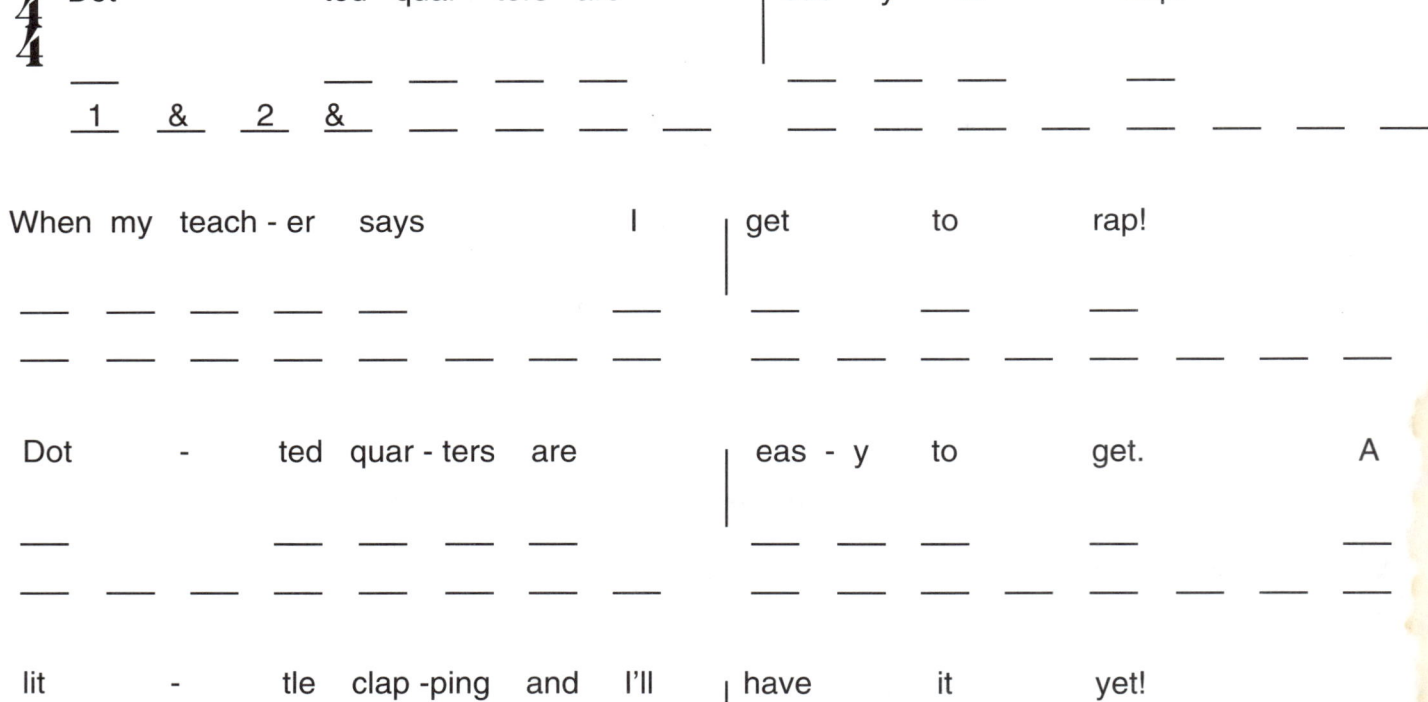

Using RH or LH C Position, IMPROVISE several
melodies that match the rhythm of Clap Rap No. 1.

C Position

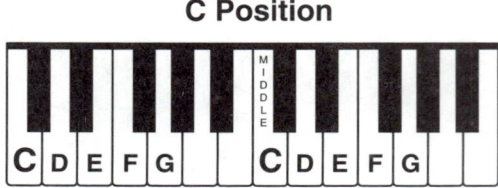

Clap Rap No. 2

$\frac{4}{4}$ Count-ing   is   a   snap   when   I | get   to   rap. | I

1   &   2   &

give   my   foot   a   tap;   I | say   the   words   and   clap!

G Position

Using RH or LH G Position, IMPROVISE several melodies that match the rhythm of Clap Rap No. 2.

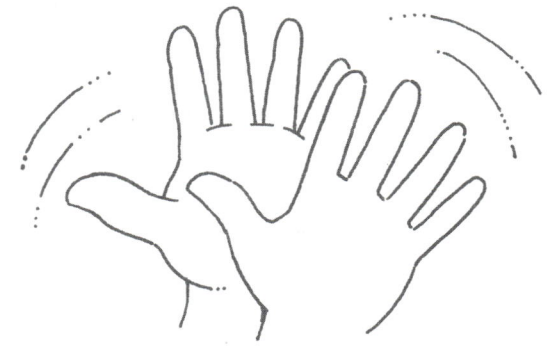

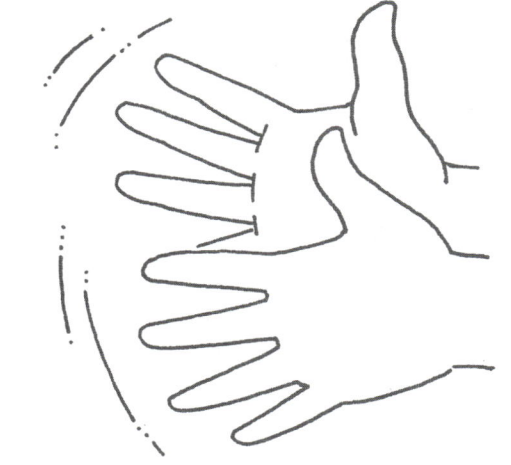

Clap Rap No. 3

LH   RH

$\frac{2}{4}$ Clap - ping   right   a - | long,   I | make   a   new | song.   I

1   &   2   &   1

play   and   count   so | well,   my | teach - er   thinks   I'm | swell!

Middle C Position

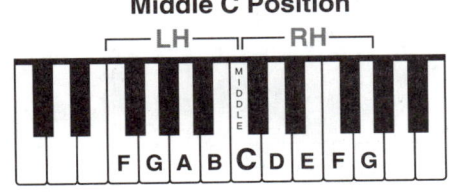

Both thumbs on MIDDLE C!

Using RH and LH Middle C Position, IMPROVISE several melodies that match the rhythm of Clap Rap No. 3.

TEACHER'S NOTE: Encourage your students to improvise melodies in each position they have learned (C, G, Middle C, Middle D, Middle D Half Step, Middle D Whole Step). These improvisations can serve as a good review of previous positions, and will give students the opportunity to explore different sounds.

TEACHER: See page 32.

Use with page 6.

Composing with Dotted Quarter Notes

1. Clap and say the words to *Famous Composers and Me!* with your teacher.
2. Using 𝅗𝅥. 𝅘𝅥 𝅗𝅥. 𝅘𝅥 and 𝅘𝅥𝅮, write the matching rhythm on the lines.
   How many beats will you need in each measure?_____
3. Using **melodic 2nds, 3rds, 4ths** and **5ths** in **C Position,** compose a melody that matches the indicated rhythm. Follow the indications for RH and LH, ending with the note C.
4. Draw a SLUR (⌢) connecting the first note of each line to the last note of each line.
5. Choose a DYNAMIC SIGN and write *f*, *mf* or *p* in the box.
6. Play your piece!

Famous Composers and Me!

Andante

RH ___

Mo - zart and | Schu - bert and | Bach   and | Brahms;

5

Men - dels-sohn, | Beeth - o - ven, | too! | They

9

LH ___

were   great com - | pos - ers when | they   were   grown | up   and   they

13

all   com-posed | ear - ly   like | you!

TEACHER: See page 32.

5

Use with page 7.

*A **PHRASE** is a MUSICAL THOUGHT or SENTENCE.*
Sometimes these musical thoughts sound like **QUESTIONS** and
sometimes they sound like **ANSWERS**.

QUESTION phrases tend to go **UP** at the end, and **ANSWER** phrases tend to go **DOWN**.
In fact, answer phrases usually end on the lowest note of the five-finger pattern
("C" in C Position). This note can also be called the KEY-NOTE.

Question and Answer Improvisation

Using **C Position,** improvise a melody for the RH with the given rhythm,
while playing the harmonic 5ths in the LH. Measures 1–4 should be a QUESTION PHRASE,
and measures 5–8 should be an ANSWER PHRASE.

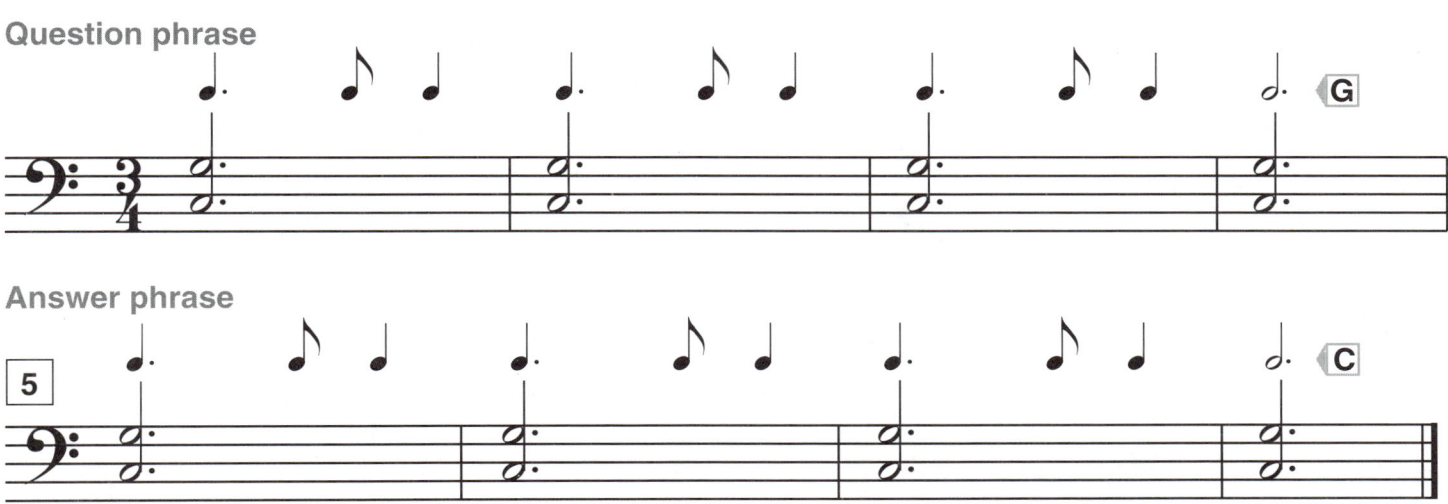

Introducing Sequence

In music, a **SEQUENCE** is the repetition of a short musical idea at another pitch.
It is usually found a 2nd or 3rd above or below the original musical idea. Play the example.

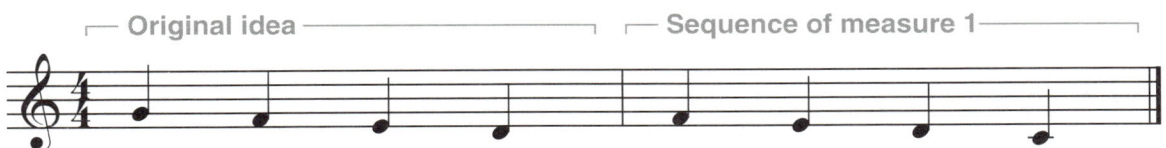

In the following example, write **SEQUENCES** where indicated, using the rhythm ♩. ♪♪
Play the example.

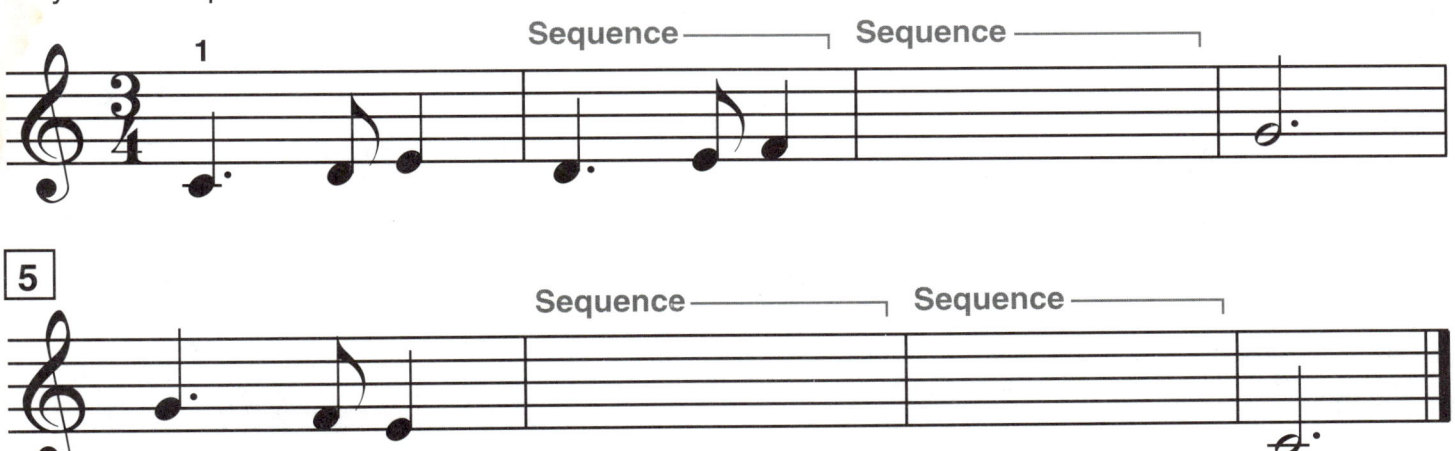

Composing with Questions, Answers and Sequences

1. Play and count the melody of *Go Composers!* several times.

2. How many beats are in each measure?_____.
   Write the correct TIME SIGNATURE under the arrows.

3. Using 𝅝 in **LH C Position,** HARMONIZE the melody with harmonic 2nds, 3rds, 4ths and 5ths.
   Note: To HARMONIZE a melody played in one hand, choose harmonic intervals for the
   accompanying hand that blend well with the melody.

4. The SEQUENCE in the 2nd line is in measure_____.

5. Play your piece!

In *Go Composers!* the first line is a QUESTION PHRASE and the second line is an
ANSWER PHRASE. The second measure is a SEQUENCE of the first measure.

Go Composers!

Measuring 6ths

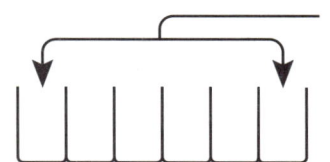

When you skip 4 white keys, the interval is a 6th.

5 FINGERS can play 6 NOTES:
C D E F G A

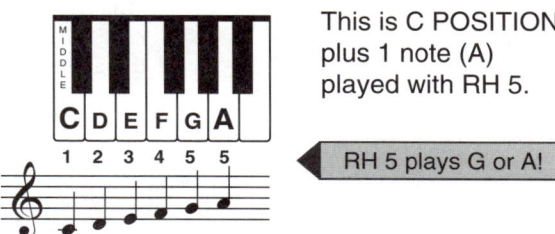

This is C POSITION plus 1 note (A) played with RH 5.

RH 5 plays G or A!

6ths are written LINE-SPACE or SPACE-LINE.

Up a 6th   Down a 6th   Up a 6th   Down a 6th

1. Using the given rhythm, clap and say the words to *Lavender's Green?*

2. Using **melodic** 2nds, 3rds, 4ths, 5ths and **6ths** in C Position, compose a melody for the RH that matches the indicated rhythm. Measures 1–4 can be a QUESTION PHRASE with measures 5–8 as its ANSWER, ending with the KEY-NOTE (C).

3. Using **harmonic** 2nds, 3rds, 4ths, 5ths and **6ths** in C Position, HARMONIZE the melody in the LH with 𝅗𝅥. and 𝅘𝅥

4. Choose DYNAMIC SIGNS and write *f*, *mf* or *p* in the appropriate places. You may also add *crescendos, diminuendos* and *accents.*

5. Draw SLURS (⌒) if you wish to indicate LEGATO or draw dots above or below the note heads (𝅘𝅥 𝅘𝅥) to indicate STACCATO.

6. Play your piece!

Lavender's Green?

8

Changing Time Signatures

Use with page 11.

In Lesson Book, Level 2, page 11, the piece *Kum-ba-yah!* uses alternating time signatures, $\frac{2}{4}$ and $\frac{4}{4}$. As you grow as a composer, you may find that not all your musical ideas fit neatly into one specific time signature. It is fun to experiment with changing time signatures.

1. On lines 3 and 4, write the correct time signature under each arrow.
2. Play the LH of *Changing Times* several times.
3. Clap and count the rhythm above the staff.
4. Using **melodic** 2nds, 3rds, 4ths, 5ths and **6ths** in C Position, compose a melody for the RH that matches the indicated rhythm.
5. Choose DYNAMIC SIGNS and write *f*, *mf* or *p* in the appropriate places. You may also add *crescendos, diminuendos* and accents.
6. Play your piece!

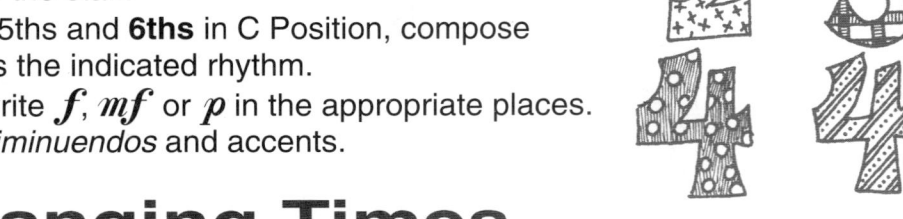

Changing Times

Improvisation with Teacher Play-Alongs!

Improvise an 8-measure melody using the indicated hand
positions as your teacher plays each accompaniment.
Listen to the 4-measure introduction to establish the tempo,
mood and style before beginning the melody.

1. Using **RH C Position one octave higher (8ᵛᵃ),**
   improvise a melody ending on the KEY-NOTE (C).

TEACHER ACCOMPANIMENT

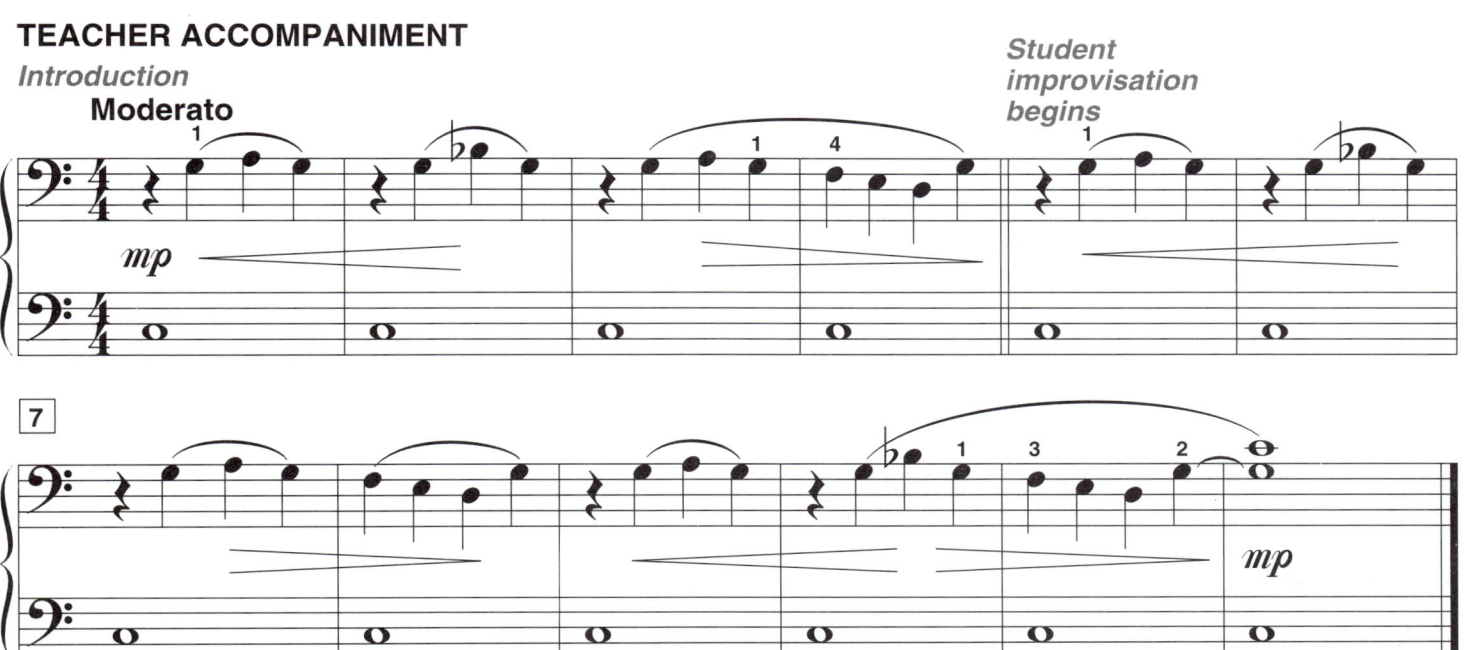

2. Using **RH G Position one octave higher (8ᵛᵃ),**
   improvise a melody ending on the KEY-NOTE (G).

TEACHER ACCOMPANIMENT

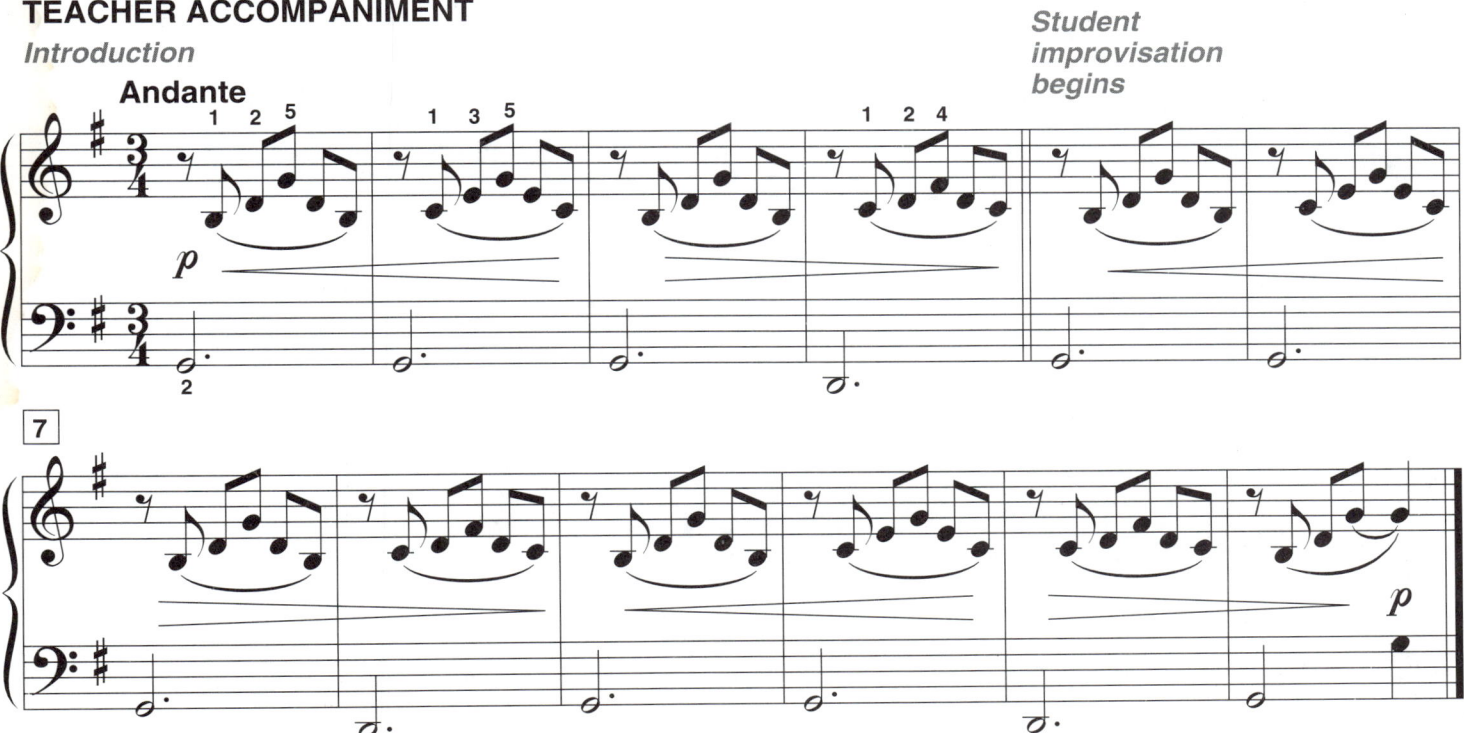

Use with page 15.

Parallel Phrases

Sometimes musical QUESTIONS and ANSWERS consist of
more than one phrase. Play the melody of the *Bell Song.*
Notice that both the QUESTION and ANSWER each have
two phrases.

Bell Song

Question

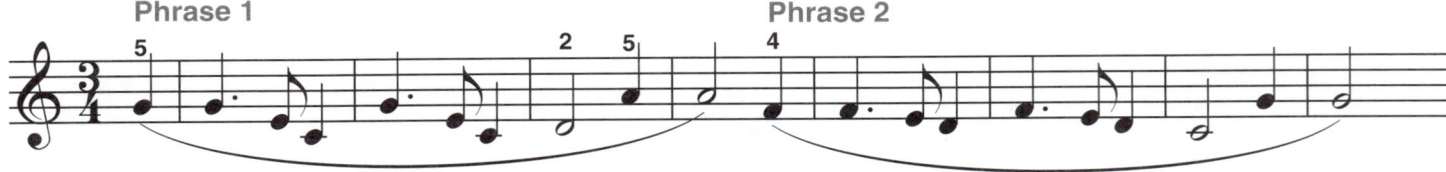

Answer

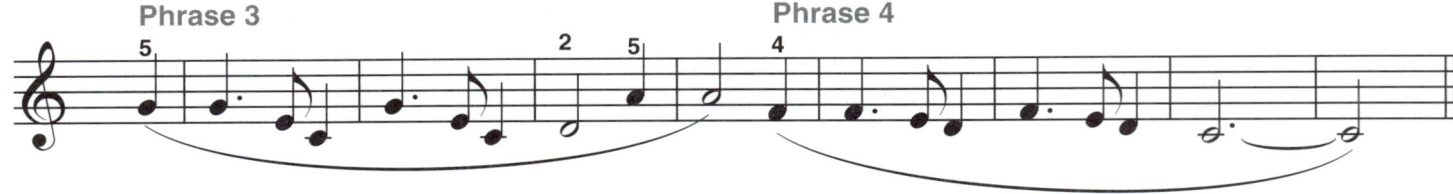

When QUESTION and ANSWER PHRASES begin the same way,
they are called PARALLEL PHRASES. The Question and Answer
Phrases of *Bell Song* are PARALLEL PHRASES.

Composing with Parallel Phrases

1. Create a PARALLEL PHRASE in *Courtly Dance* on page 11 by copying
   the same notes from *Phrase 1* onto the line labeled *Phrase 3.*

2. Play the LH of *Courtly Dance.*

3. Using **melodic** 2nds, 3rds, 4ths, 5ths and **6ths** in **G Position,**
   compose a melody for *Phrase 2* that extends the question begun in *Phrase 1.*

4. Using **melodic** 2nds, 3rds, 4ths, 5ths and **6ths** in **G Position,**
   compose a melody for *Phrase 4* that extends the answer begun in *Phrase 3.*
   End this phrase on the KEY-NOTE (G).

5. Write a TEMPO MARK that best suits your piece in the box.
   Some suggestions follow:

   Allegro = Quickly, happily   **Moderato** = Moderately
   Andante = Moving along, walking tempo   **Adagio** = Slow

6. Choose DYNAMIC SIGNS and write *f*, *mf*, or *p* in the appropriate places.
   You may also add *crescendos, diminuendos* and *accents.*

7. Use the appropriate indications for LEGATO (⌒) and STACCATO (♩̇ ♩).

8. Play your piece!

Courtly Dance

Question
Phrase 1

5 Phrase 2

9 Answer
Phrase 3

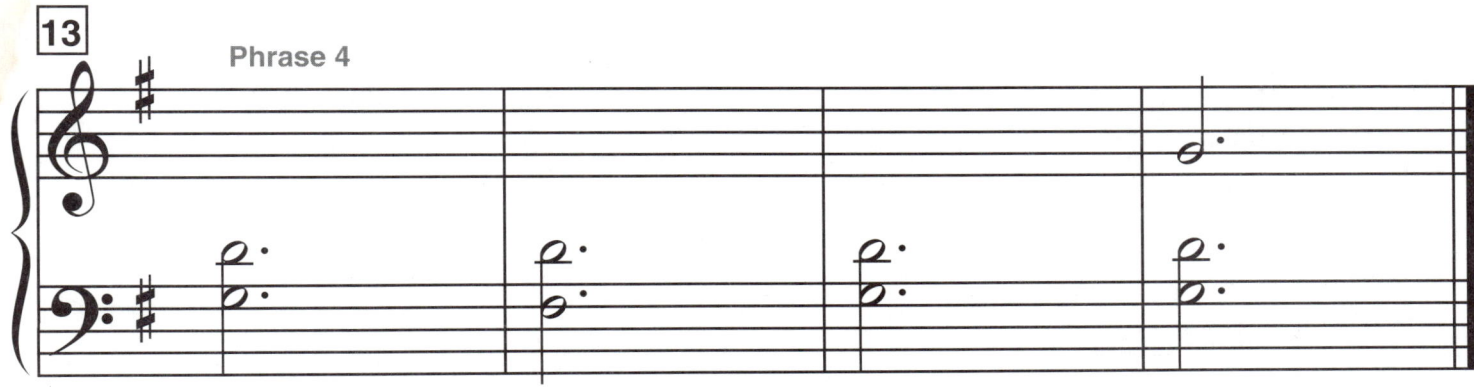

13 Phrase 4

Use with pages 16–17.

Three-Part Form—ABA

(A) Pieces of music are often divided into sections. The way the sections are arranged determines the FORM of the piece. *Lone Star Waltz* has three sections. The first section (measures 1–8) is called **"A."** Write a big **"A"** above measure 1.

(B) Since a new musical idea begins in meas. 9, it will be considered a new section. The second section (measures 9–16) is called **"B." B** sections provide CONTRAST to a piece of music. Write a big **"B"** above measure 9.

(A) Notice that, because of the *D.C. al Fine,* you play section **"A"** again. Therefore, the FORM of *Lone Star Waltz* is a three-part form known as **ABA.**

Unity and Variety

Pieces of music contain elements of UNITY *(musical ideas that are the same or similar)* and elements of VARIETY *(musical ideas that are different).* One of the ways composers create UNITY is through the use of **REPETITION** *(repeating a musical idea).*

* In the **A** section of *Lone Star Waltz,* notice how REPETITION is used when the RH in the second line repeats the RH in the first line.

One of the ways composers create VARIETY is through the use of **VARIATION** *(changing some elements of a musical idea while retaining others).* VARIATION is a compositional technique that combines elements of UNITY and VARIETY.

* In *Lone Star Waltz,* notice how the **B** section provides VARIETY. Within the **B** section, the LH in measures 17–24 contains a **VARIATION** of the melody found in the RH in measures 9–16.

Lone Star Waltz

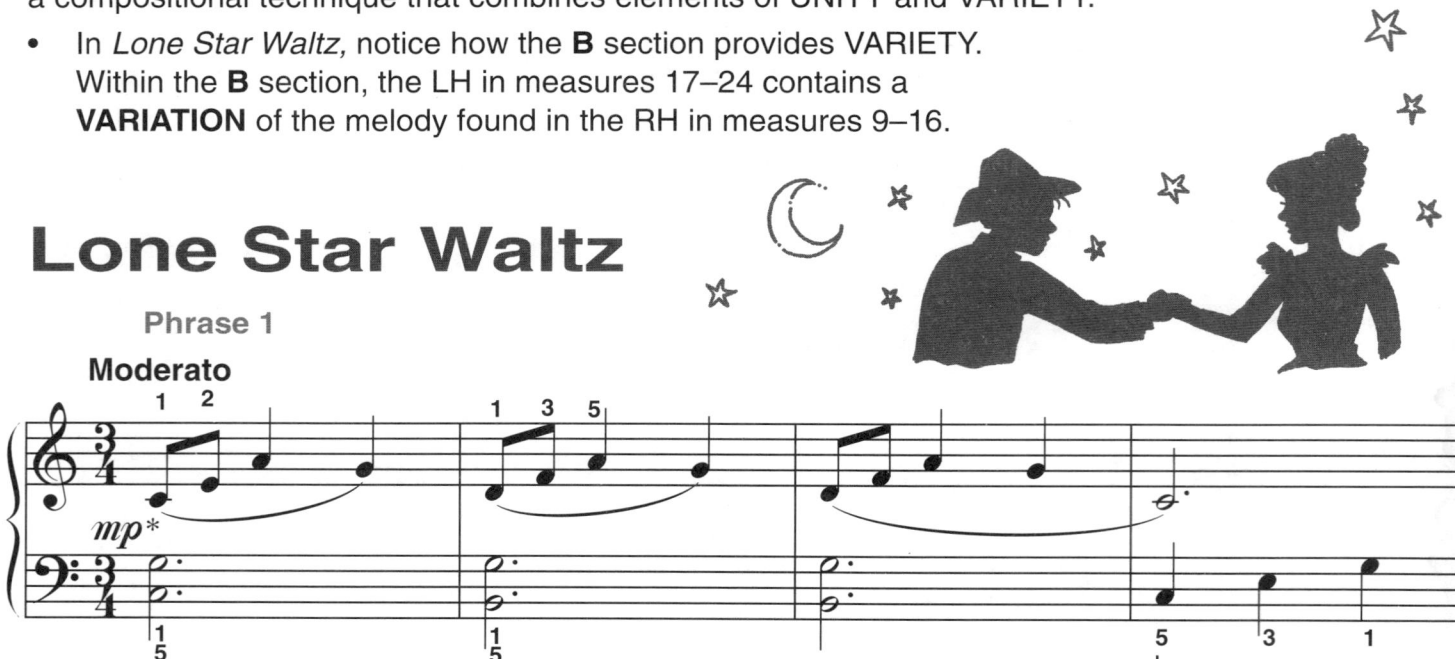

*mp = mezzo piano, moderately soft.

Phrase 3

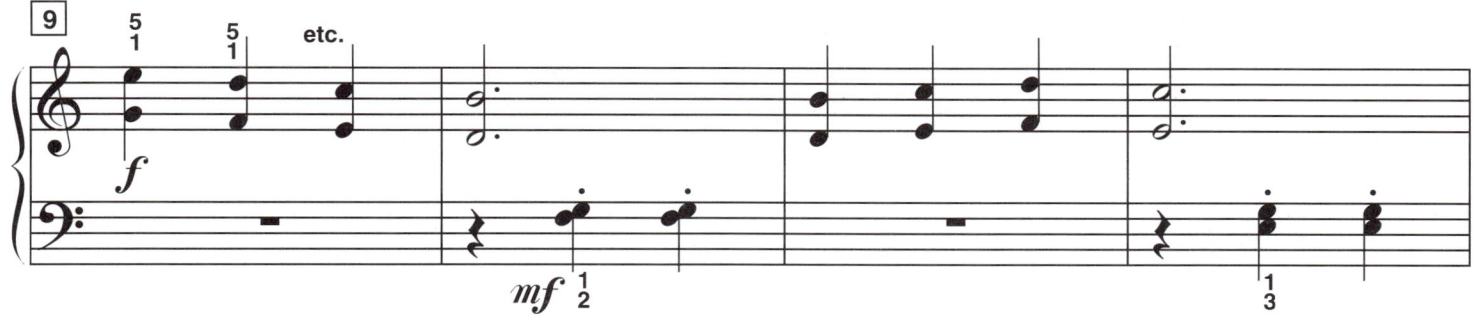

REPETITION of Phrase 3

VARIATION of Phrase 3

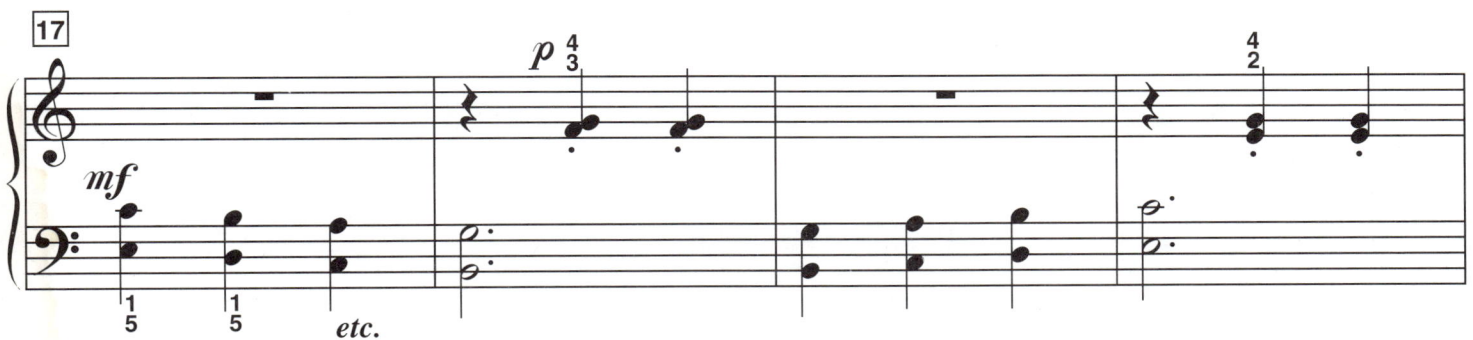

REPETITION of VARIATION

D.C. al Fine

Composing in ABA Form

Use with page 19.

1. Play and count the first and third lines of *Music Box Waltz* several times.

2. Using **melodic** 2nds, 3rds, 4ths, 5ths and 6ths in the RH, complete the melody on lines 2 and 4. On line 2, compose a PARALLEL ANSWER PHRASE to line 1. A PARALLEL ANSWER PHRASE begins the same way as its QUESTION, but ends on the KEY-NOTE (C). On line 4, compose a SEQUENCE similar to line 3 beginning on the given notes.

3. Using **harmonic** 2nds, 3rds, 4ths, 5ths and 6ths in the LH, HARMONIZE your phrases. G should always be the top note of your interval.

4. Choose DYNAMIC SIGNS and write *f*, *mf*, *mp* or *p* in the appropriate places. You may also add *crescendos, diminuendos* and *accents*.

5. Use the appropriate indications for LEGATO (⌒) and STACCATO (' .).

6. Play your piece!

Music Box Waltz

My "Note"book

Composers frequently keep notebooks to record their musical ideas. Beethoven was known to carry a sketchbook with him always to record his musical inspirations whenever they occured. As you experiment at the piano, you may wish to record your musical ideas just as the great composers have done. Some of these ideas may serve as inspirations for new compositions. On the next few pages, you will be introduced to some new compositional techniques to help you expand your compositions through variation. Use this page to record any additional ideas you may have.

Use with pages 20–21.

Creating Variety

There are many ways to vary your musical ideas. The examples below show VARIATION TECHNIQUES frequently used by composers. Play the original musical idea.

Original Musical Idea

Varying the Melody

As you play the melodic variations below, notice that the melody changes, but the rhythm remains the same. Compose your own MELODIC VARIATION on the staff.

Melodic Variation 1

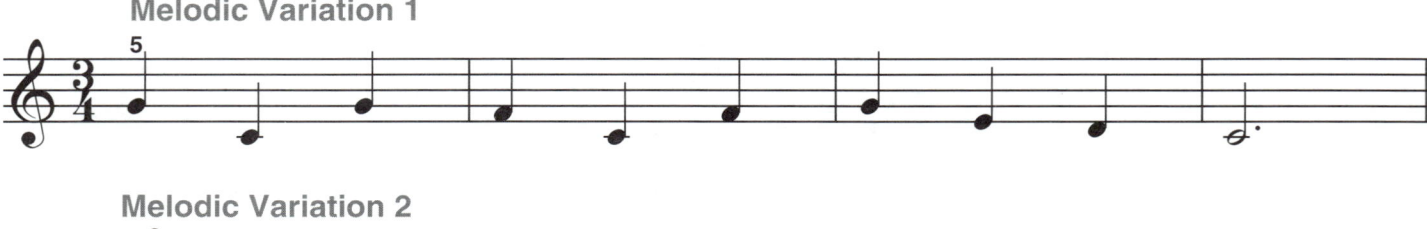

Melodic Variation 2

MY MELODIC VARIATION

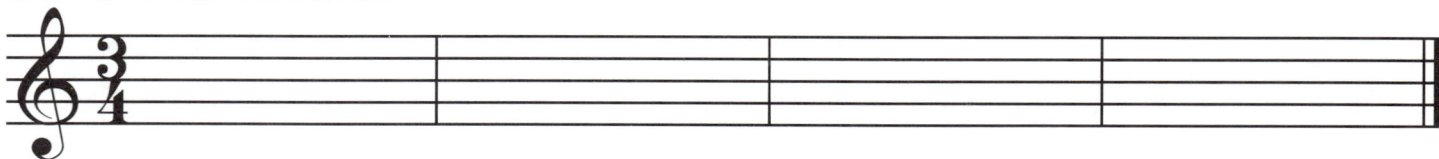

Varying the Rhythm

As you play the rhythmic variations below, notice that the rhythm changes, but the melody notes remain the same. Compose your own RHYTHMIC VARIATION on the staff.

Rhythmic Variation 1

Rhythmic Variation 2

MY RHYTHMIC VARIATION

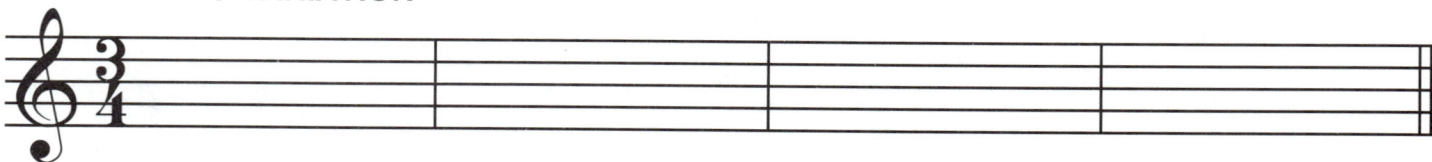

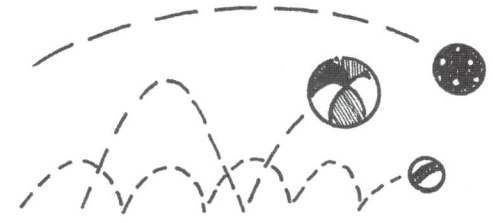

Varying the Melody and the Rhythm

As you play the melodic and rhythmic variations below, notice that changes were made in both the melody and the rhythm. Combine MELODIC and RHYTHMIC VARIATION TECHNIQUES to create a variation on the staff.

Melodic and Rhythmic Variation 1

Melodic and Rhythmic Variation 2

MY MELODIC AND RHYTHMIC VARIATION

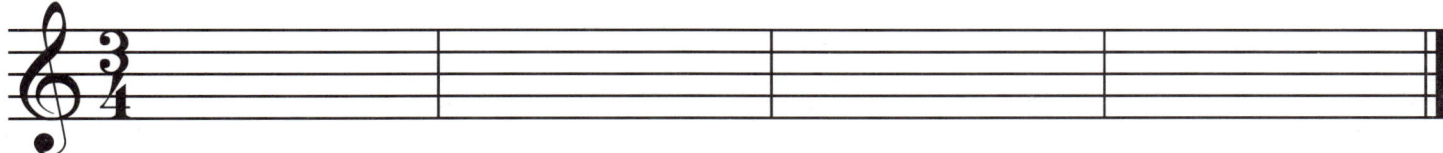

Varying the Dynamics

Play the original musical idea below several times. Each time you play use a different dynamic: *ff*, *f*, *mf*, *mp*, *p* and *pp*. Notice that VARYING THE DYNAMIC LEVEL changes the CHARACTER or MOOD of the music.

NEW DYNAMIC SIGNS

ff **Fortissimo** very loud

pp **Pianissimo** very soft

Original Musical Idea

Varying the Touch

Play the example above using a LEGATO touch throughout; play it again using a STACCATO touch throughout. Then, experiment with combinations of these touches while adding ACCENTS. Notice that VARYING THE TOUCH also changes the CHARACTER or MOOD of the music.

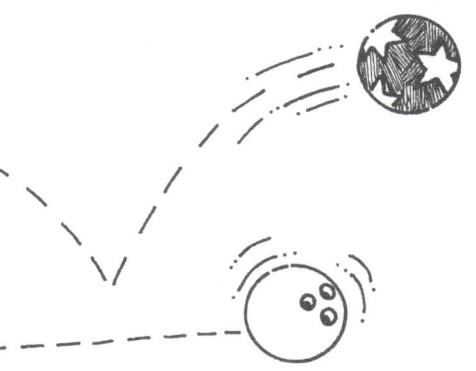

Use with page 23.

Measuring 7ths

When you skip 5 white keys, the interval is an **7th.**

7ths are written LINE-LINE or SPACE-SPACE.

Improvisation with Teacher Play-Alongs!

Improvise an 8-measure melody in C Major (RH one octave above Middle C) using 2nds, 3rds, 4ths, 5ths, 6ths and **7ths** as your teacher plays each accompaniment. Listen to the 4-measure introduction to establish the tempo, mood and style before beginning the melody. End on the KEY-NOTE (C).

TEACHER ACCOMPANIMENT

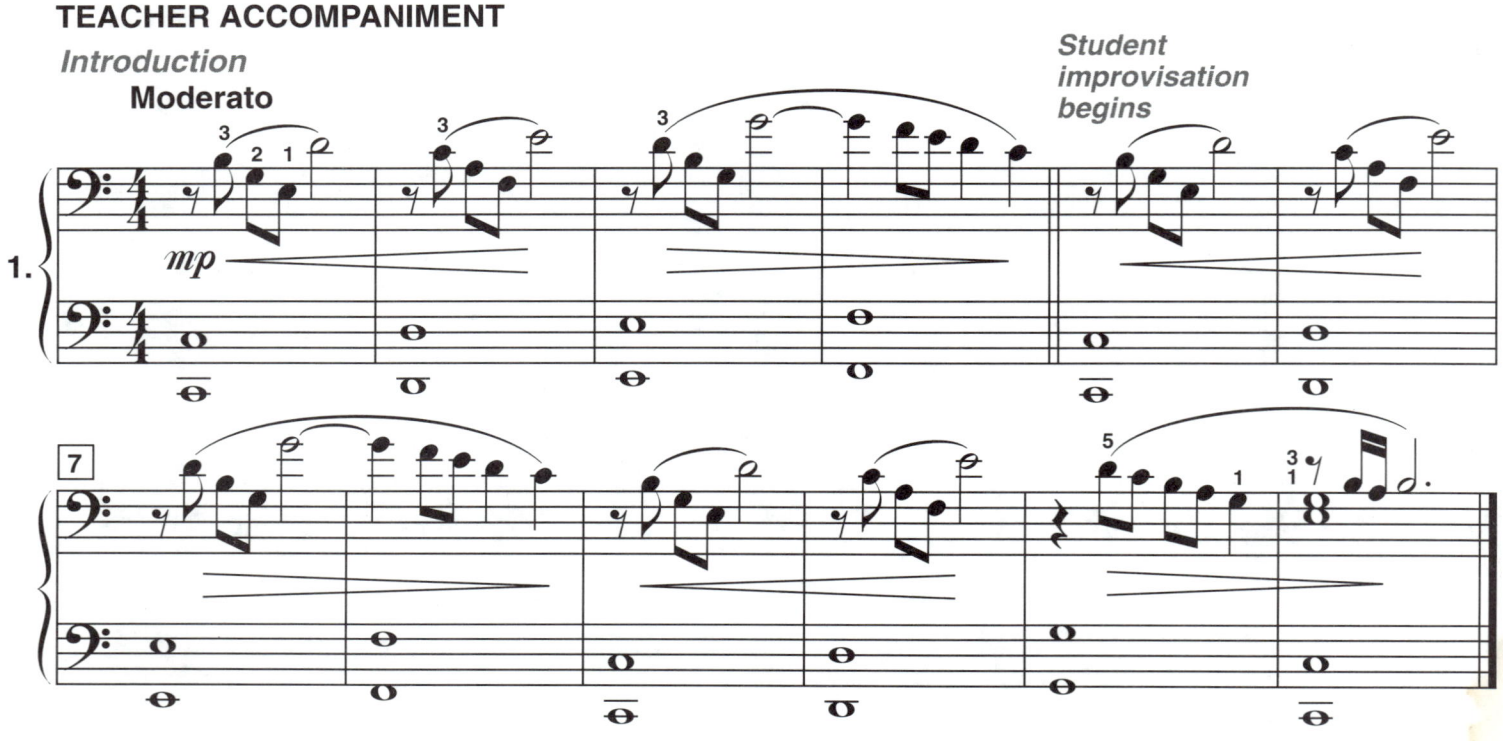

TEACHER ACCOMPANIMENT

Use with page 23.

Composing With Melodic and Rhythmic Variations

1. Play and count the given melody and accompaniment of *Spring Day* several times.
2. Beginning with measure 5, use 2nds, 3rds, 4ths, 5ths,6ths and **7ths** to complete the melody of *Spring Day*. Follow the indications for **Melodic Variation, Melodic and Rhythmic Variation,** and **Rhythmic Variation.**
3. Choose DYNAMIC SIGNS and write $\textit{ff}$, $\textit{f}$, $\textit{mf}$, $\textit{mp}$, $\textit{p}$, or $\textit{pp}$ in the appropriate places.
4. Use the appropriate indications for LEGATO (⌣) and STACCATO ( ).
5. Play your piece!

Spring Day

Moderato
Original musical idea

5 MELODIC VARIATION: Melody changes, rhythm remains the same.

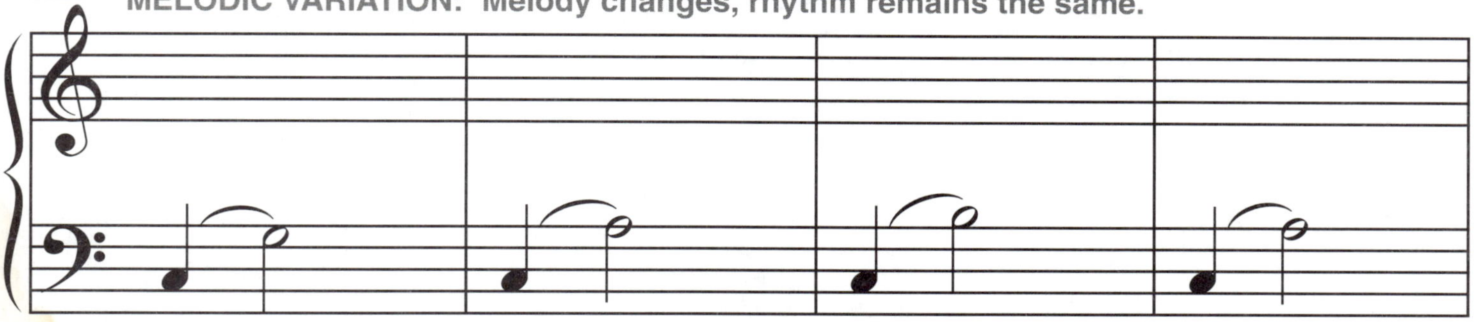

9 MELODIC AND RHYTHMIC VARIATION: Melody and rhythm change.

13 RHYTHMIC VARIATION (of measures 1–2): Rhythm changes, melody remains the same.

Use with page 25.

C Major Scale

Ascending C Major Scale

LH 5 4 3 2 1 3 2 1

Descending C Major Scale

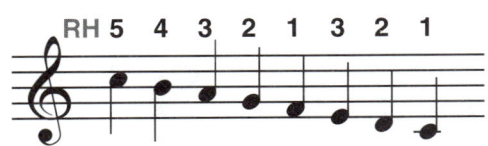

RH 5 4 3 2 1 3 2 1

> ### 8va
>
> The sign **8va** placed over the notes means *play the notes one octave (8 notes) higher than written.*

1. Play the first line of *A Prelude to My Success* several times.
2. The tools that composers use to develop and expand their musical ideas into larger phrases or even entire pieces are called COMPOSITIONAL TECHNIQUES.

   Using notes from the C MAJOR SCALE, complete *A Prelude to My Success* ending on the KEY-NOTE (C). Try using some of the COMPOSITIONAL TECHNIQUES you have learned so far:

QUESTION AND ANSWER PHRASES (Page 5)	SEQUENCE (Page 5)
PARALLEL PHRASES (Page 10)	REPETITION (Page 12)
ABA FORM (Page 12)	VARIATION (Pages 16–17)

3. Use the **8va SIGN** if you want to play any line up an octave.
4. Write the TEMPO MARK that best suits your piece *(Allegro, Moderato, Andante or Adagio)* in the box.
5. Choose DYNAMIC SIGNS and write *ff*, *f*, *mf*, *mp*, *p*, or *pp* in the appropriate places. You may also add *crescendos, diminuendos* and *accents.*
6. Use the appropriate indications for LEGATO (⌢) and STACCATO (′ .).
7. Play your piece!

A Prelude to My Success

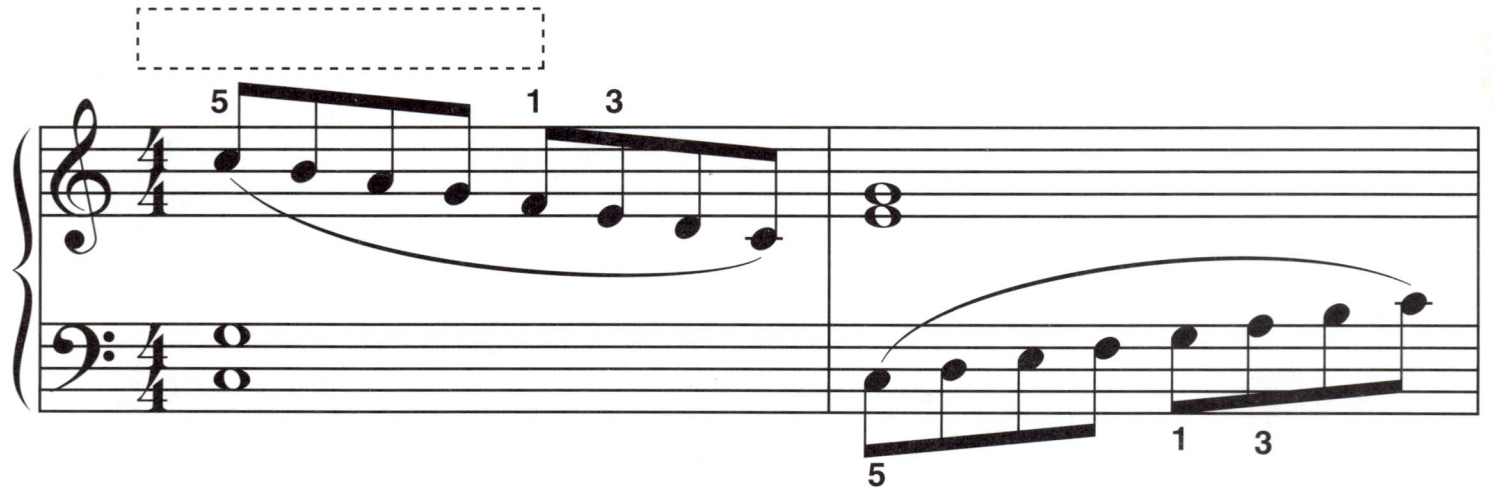

3

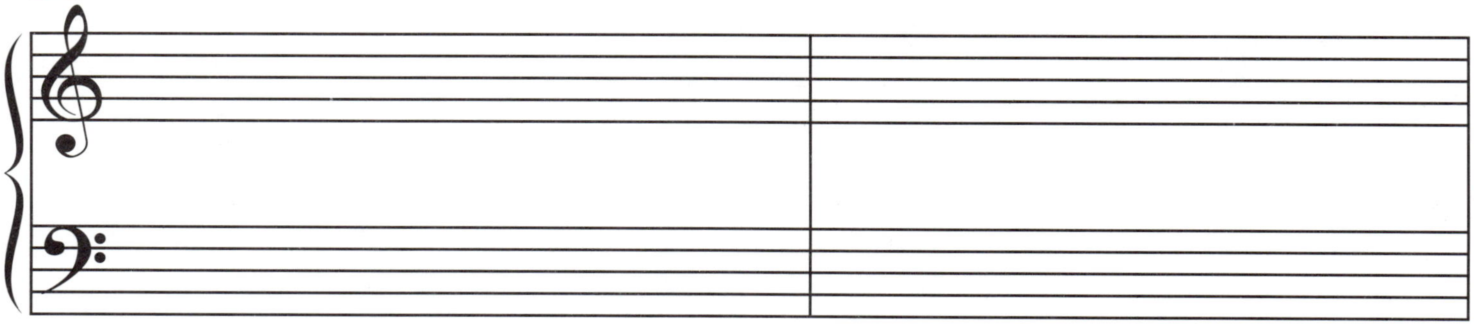

5

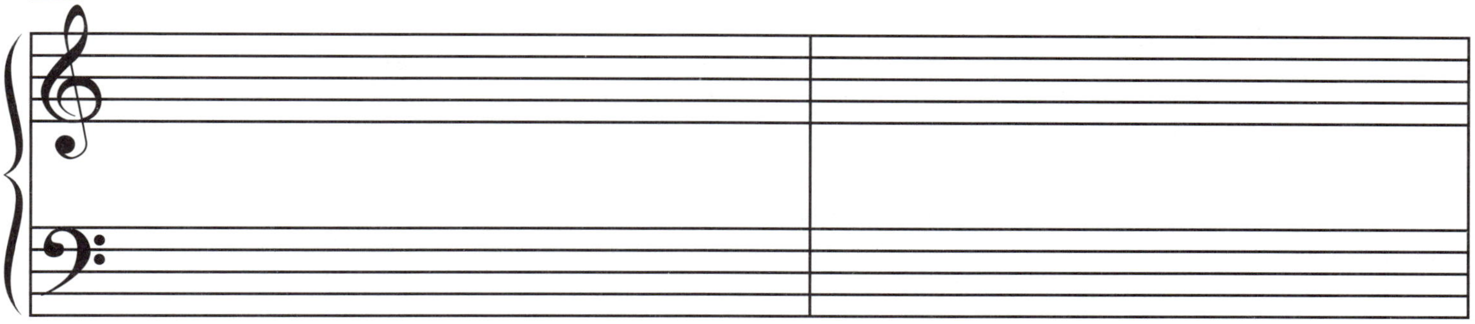

7

Improvising with the C Major Scale

1. The counting is given at the beginning of this example.
   Write the counting (using 1 & 2 & 3 & 4 &)
   for the remainder of the example.

2. Clap and count the given rhythm several times.

3. Using the notes of the C MAJOR SCALE, improvise several melodies to
   go with the given rhythm, first in the RH, then in the LH, beginning with
   your 5th finger. The melodies can go up or down, but remember to use
   the correct scale fingerings.

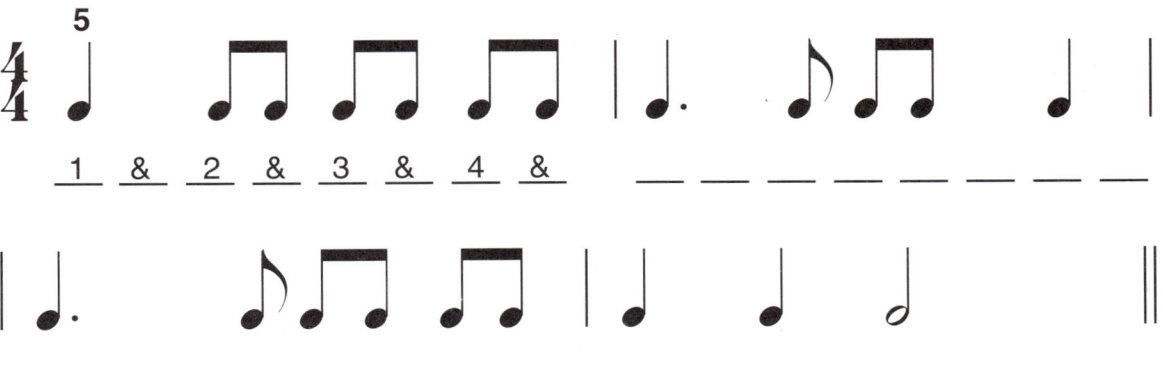

1 & 2 & 3 & 4 &

Use with page 27.

Measuring Octaves (8ths)

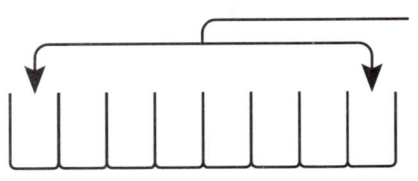

When you skip 6 white keys,
the interval is a **OCTAVE**.

Octaves are written LINE-SPACE or SPACE-LINE.

Up an Octave Down an Octave   Up an Octave Down an Octave

1. Draw the correct TIME SIGNATURE in the appropriate places of *I Can-Can*.

2. Play and count the LH accompaniment.

3. Using notes from the C MAJOR SCALE, compose an eight-measure melody that blends well with the LH. Use the interval of an octave at least once in your melody. End with the KEY-NOTE (C).

4. Choose DYNAMIC SIGNS and write *ff*, *f*, *mf*, *mp*, or *pp* in the appropriate places. You may also add *crescendos, diminuendos* and accents.

5. Use the appropriate indications for LEGATO (⌒) and STACCATO (⸭).

6. Play your piece!

I Can-Can

Allegro

Transposition

To TRANSPOSE is to write or play the same music in a different key.
Play examples **A** and **B** below. Notice that the INTERVALS in **A** are
exactly the same as the INTERVALS in **B**.

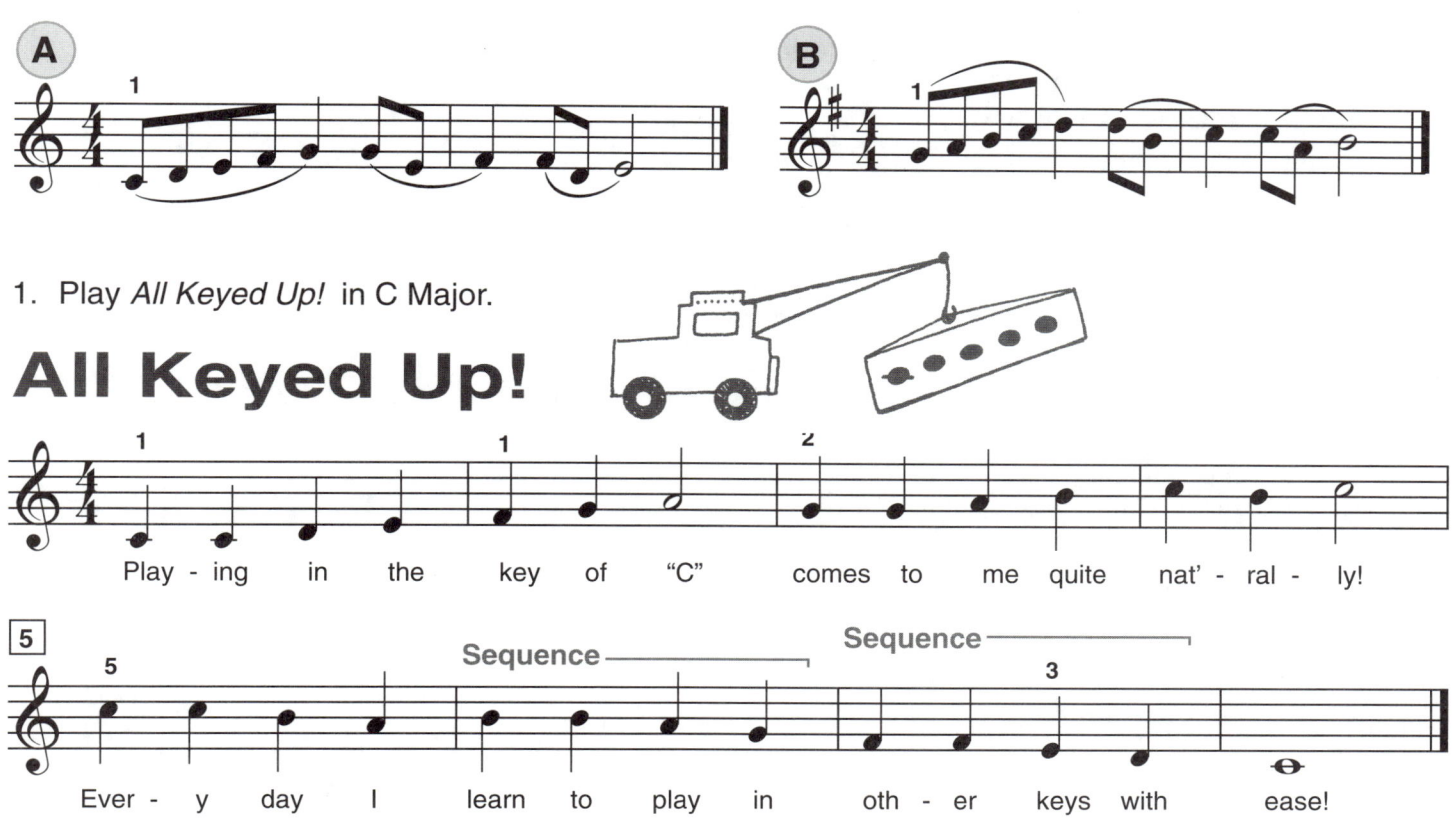

1. Play *All Keyed Up!* in C Major.

All Keyed Up!

Play - ing in the key of "C" comes to me quite nat' - ral - ly!

Ever - y day I learn to play in oth - er keys with ease!

2. Finish TRANSPOSING *All Keyed Up!* to G Major.
   Begin on the given pitches, and use the exact pattern
   of intervals found in *All Keyed Up!* in C Major.

3. Copy the fingering given in *All Keyed Up!* in C Major
   into the appropriate places in *All Keyed Up!* in G Major.

4. Play *All Keyed Up!* in G Major.

Ascending G Major Scale

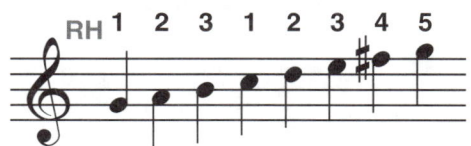

Descending G Major Scale

All Keyed Up!

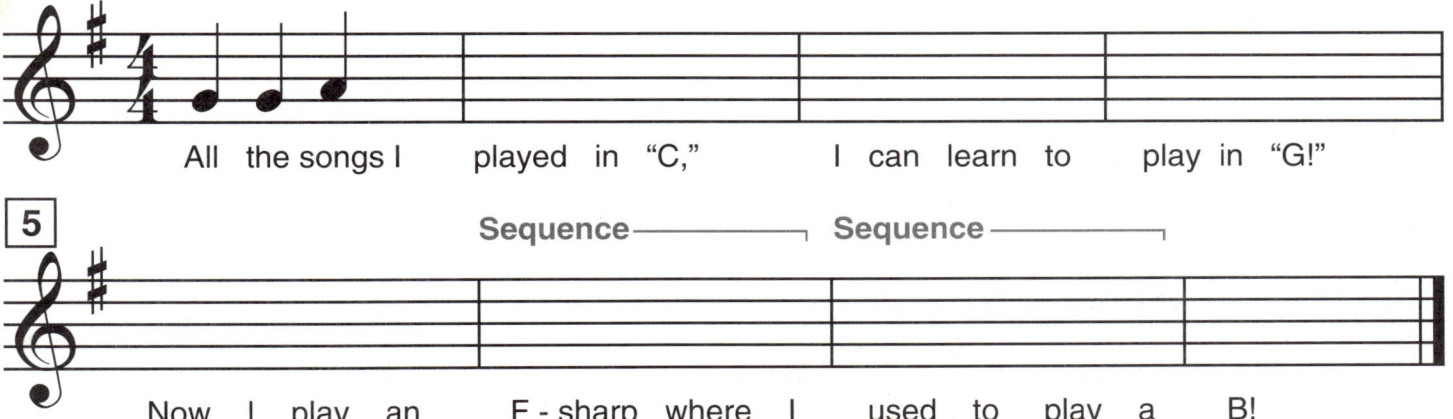

All the songs I played in "C," I can learn to play in "G!"

Now I play an F - sharp where I used to play a B!

Use with page 31.

Triads

1. Draw the correct TIME SIGNATURE in the appropriate places of *RH Triads, LH Melody*.

2. Play and count the RH triads.

3. Beginning with your LH in G Position, compose a melody that blends well with the RH accompaniment. You may wish to move your LH up or down a step when your RH moves up or down a step. Begin and end with the KEY-NOTE (G).

4. Choose DYNAMIC SIGNS and write *ff*, *f*, *mf*, *mp*, or *pp* in the appropriate places. You may also add *crescendos, diminuendos* and accents.

5. Use the appropriate indications for LEGATO (⌒) and STACCATO (♩. ♩).

6. Play your piece!

A TRIAD IS A 3-NOTE CHORD.

THE THREE NOTES OF A TRIAD ARE:

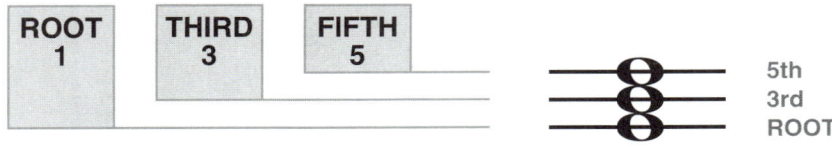

The ROOT is the note from which the triad gets its name.
The ROOT of a C triad is C.

TRIADS IN **ROOT POSITION** (WITH THE ROOT AT THE BOTTOM) ALWAYS LOOK LIKE THIS:

Triads may be built on any note of any scale.

TRIADS in C

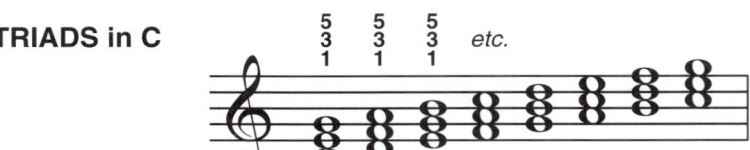

RH Triads, LH Melody

Allegro moderato

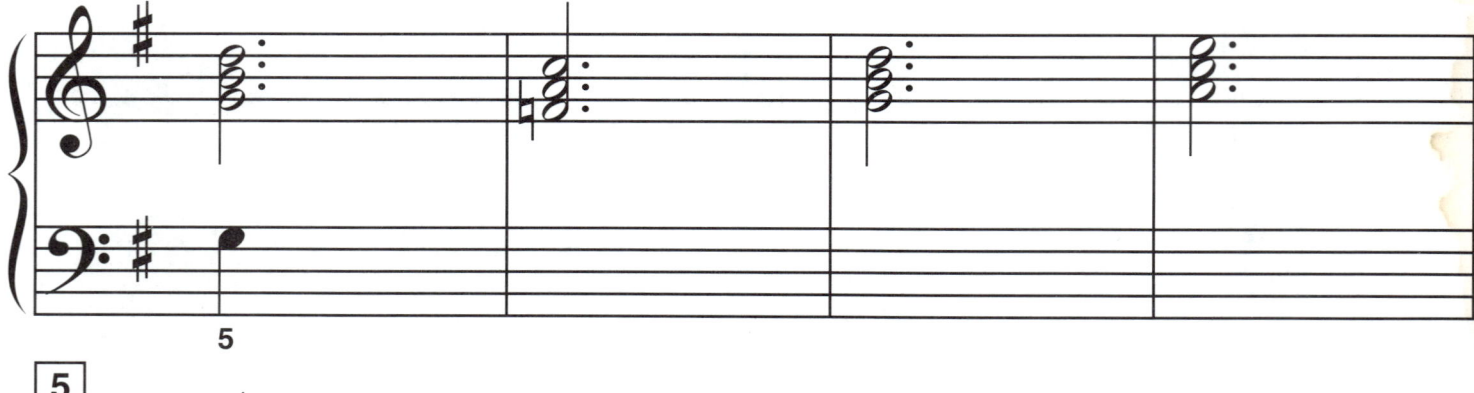

More Triads

TRIADS in C

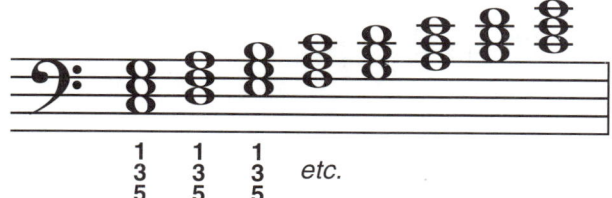

```
1    1    1
3    3    3    etc.
5    5    5
```

1. Play and count the LH of *LH Triads, RH Melody.*

2. Using the notes of the RH C MAJOR SCALE, compose a melody that blends well with the accompaniment. Begin and end with the KEY-NOTE (C). Notice that the RH is to be played **8ᵛᵃ.**

3. Write the TEMPO MARK that best suits your piece *(Allegro, Moderato, Andante* or *Adagio)* in the box.

4. Choose DYNAMIC SIGNS and write ***ff***, ***f***, *mf*, *mp*, or *pp* in the appropriate places. You may also add *crescendos, diminuendos* and accents.

5. Use the appropriate indications for LEGATO (‿) and STACCATO ( ).

6. Play your piece!

LH Triads, RH Melody

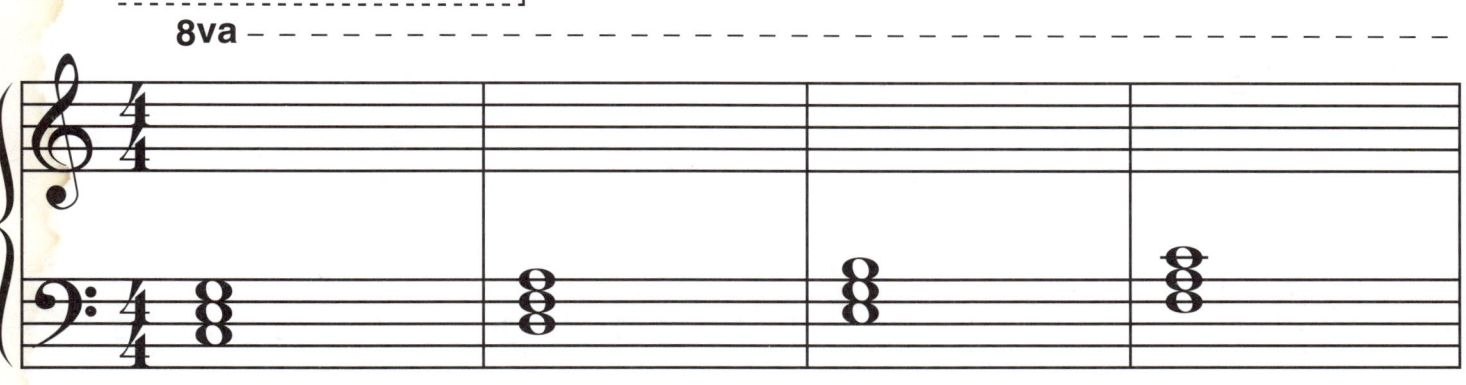

Use with page 34.

The Primary Triads

The 3 most important triads in any key are those built on the 1st, 4th & 5th notes of the scale. These are called the **PRIMARY TRIADS.**

The chords are identified by the Roman numerals **I, IV & V** (1, 4 & 5).

In the key of C MAJOR, the **I** CHORD (1 chord) is the C TRIAD.

The **IV** CHORD (4 chord) is the F TRIAD. The **V** CHORD (5 chord) is the G TRIAD.

The KEY SIGNATURE of the key of C MAJOR has no sharps or flats.

THE PRIMARY TRIADS IN C MAJOR:

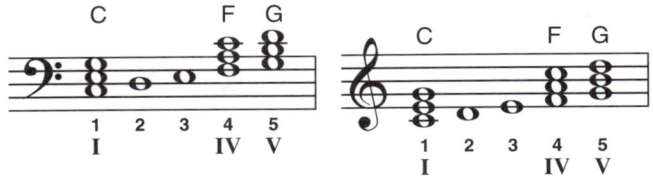

Write the three notes of each PRIMARY TRIAD in C Major above the Roman numerals:

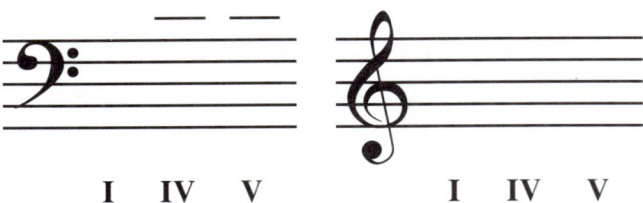

I   IV   V   I   IV   V

1. Using only the notes of the indicated PRIMARY TRIADS in C Major, complete *Trying Out Triads*. Note that measures 3–4 are a SEQUENCE of the musical idea presented in measures 1–2; the triads that follow should create a similar sequence.

2. Choose DYNAMIC SIGNS and write *ff*, *f*, *mf*, *mp*, or *pp* in the appropriate places. You may also add *crescendos, diminuendos* and *accents.*

3. Use the appropriate indications for LEGATO (⌢) and STACCATO (˙).

4. Play your piece!

Trying Out Triads

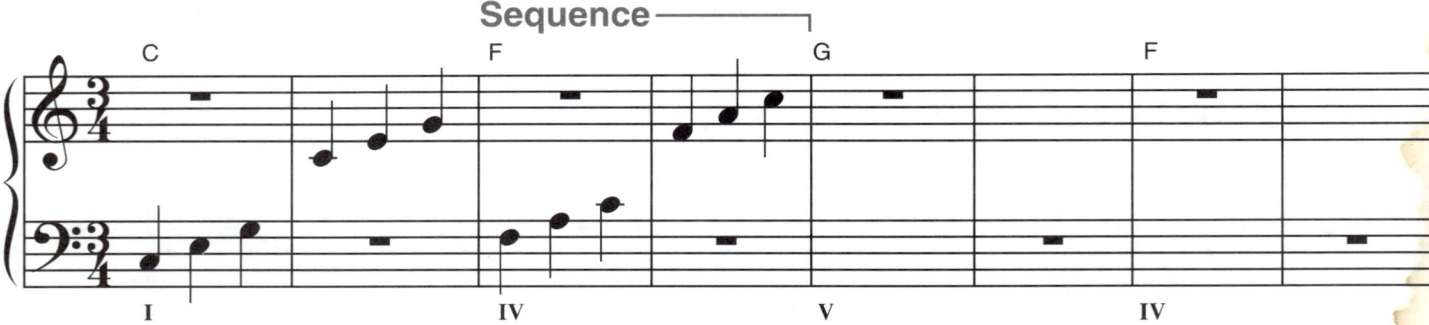

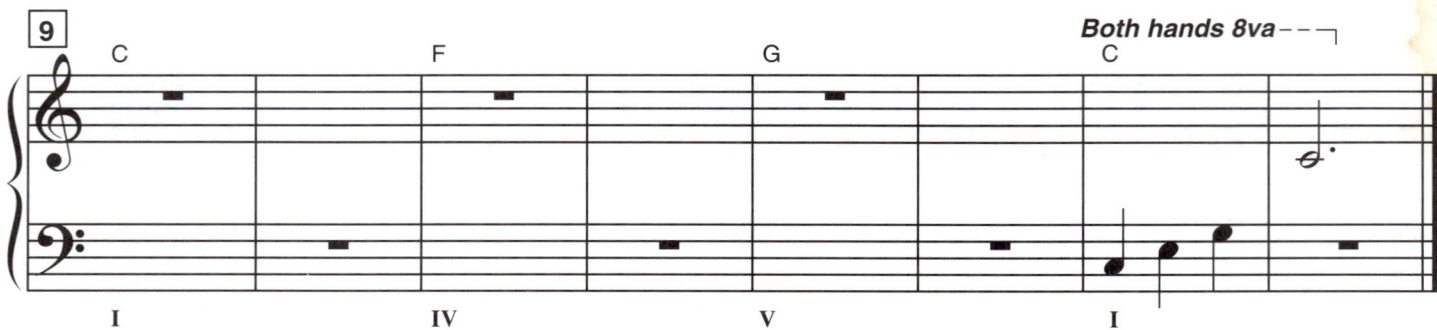

When we change from one chord to another, we call this a CHORD PROGRESSION. Much of the popular music written today uses CHORD PROGRESSIONS based on the PRIMARY TRIADS. In fact, many songs you may hear on the radio use only PRIMARY TRIADS!

The CHORD PROGRESSION of *Trying Out Triads* is: I – IV – V – IV – I – IV – V – I
                                                     (C – F – G – F – C – F – G – C)

Experiment with the PRIMARY TRIADS, and create your own CHORD PROGRESSIONS!

The V⁷ Chord

In many pieces a **V⁷ CHORD** is used instead of a **V** Triad.
To make a **V⁷** chord, a note an interval of a 7th above the root is
added to the **V** triad.

To make chord progressions easier to play and sound better, the **IV**
and **V⁷** may be played in other positions by moving one or more of
the higher chord tones down an octave.

1. Play and count the melody of *A Primary Impression* several times.

2. HARMONIZE the melody using **I, IV** and **V⁷** chords in **C Major.**
   Experiment with each chord in every measure, and choose the chords
   that are the most "harmonious." Follow the indications for o ♩ and ♪

3. Write the appropriate CHORD SYMBOLS (**I, IV** and **V⁷**) in the boxes below each measure.

4. Choose DYNAMIC SIGNS and write *ff*, *f*, *mf*, *mp*, or *pp*
   in the appropriate places. You may also add *crescendos, diminuendos* and accents.

5. Play your piece!

A Primary Impression

Moderate blues tempo*

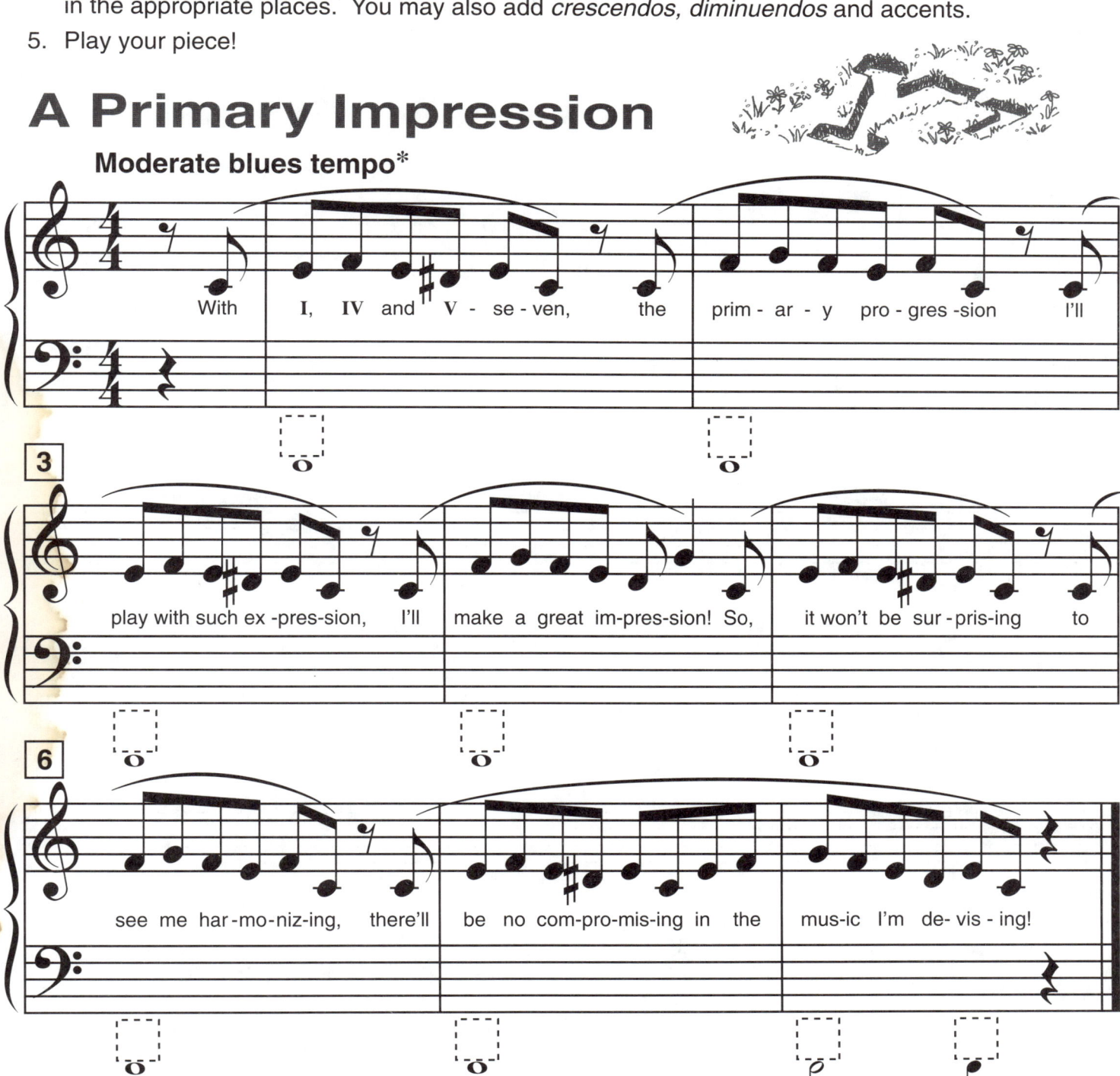

With | I, IV and V - se - ven, the | prim - ar - y pro - gres -sion I'll

3 play with such ex -pres-sion, I'll | make a great im-pres-sion! So, | it won't be sur -pris-ing to

6 see me har-mo-niz-ing, there'll | be no com-pro-mis-ing in the | mus-ic I'm de- vis - ing!

*OPTIONAL: Eighth notes may be played in long-short pairs.

Use with page 39.

The Primary Chords in G Major

The KEY SIGNATURE of the KEY OF G MAJOR is ONE SHARP (♯).

The 3 PRIMARY CHORDS
in the key of G MAJOR are:

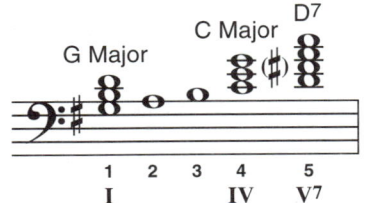

The IV and V7 Chords are moved to lower
positions, for smooth and easy progressions:

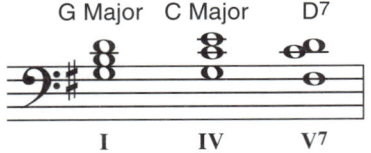

1. Play and count the given melody and accompaniment to *Gee, I'm Blue.*

2. Complete the RH melody. Experiment with B♭ and B♮ in your melody. B♭ sounds especially "bluesy" with the **IV CHORD,** much like the F♮ sounds "bluesy" with the **I CHORD.** End with the KEY-NOTE (G).

3. Write the TEMPO MARK that best suits your piece *(Allegro, Moderato, Andante* or *Adagio)* in the appropriate place.

4. Choose DYNAMIC SIGNS and write *ff*, *f*, *mf*, *mp*, or *pp*
   in the appropriate places. You may also add *crescendos, diminuendos* and *accents.*

5. Use the appropriate indications for LEGATO (⌣) and STACCATO (˙).

6. Play your piece!

Gee, I'm Blue

*OPTIONAL: Eighth notes may be played in long-short pairs.

Block Chords and Broken Chords

Chords are often used as follows:

BLOCK CHORDS (all notes together).   **BROKEN CHORDS** (one note at a time).

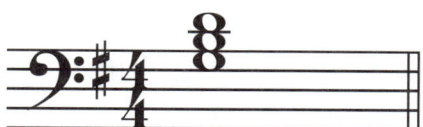   

1. This is the G Major KEY SIGNATURE:
   Copy it in the boxes at the beginning of each staff.

2. Play and count the BLOCK AND BROKEN CHORDS given for the LH below.

3. Using the notes of the G MAJOR SCALE, write a melody that blends well with the accompaniment. End with the KEY-NOTE (G). You may wish to repeat measures 1–2 in measures 5–6 to create a PARALLEL PHRASE.

4. Choose DYNAMIC SIGNS and write *ff*, *f*, *mf*, *mp*, or *pp* in the appropriate places. You may also add *crescendos, diminuendos* and accents.

5. Use the appropriate indications for LEGATO (⌒) and STACCATO (⸱ ⸱).

6. Add a title that describes the music you have composed and play your piece!

Title: _____

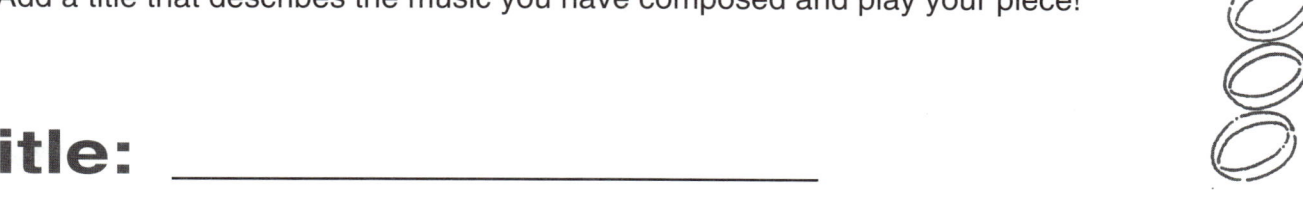

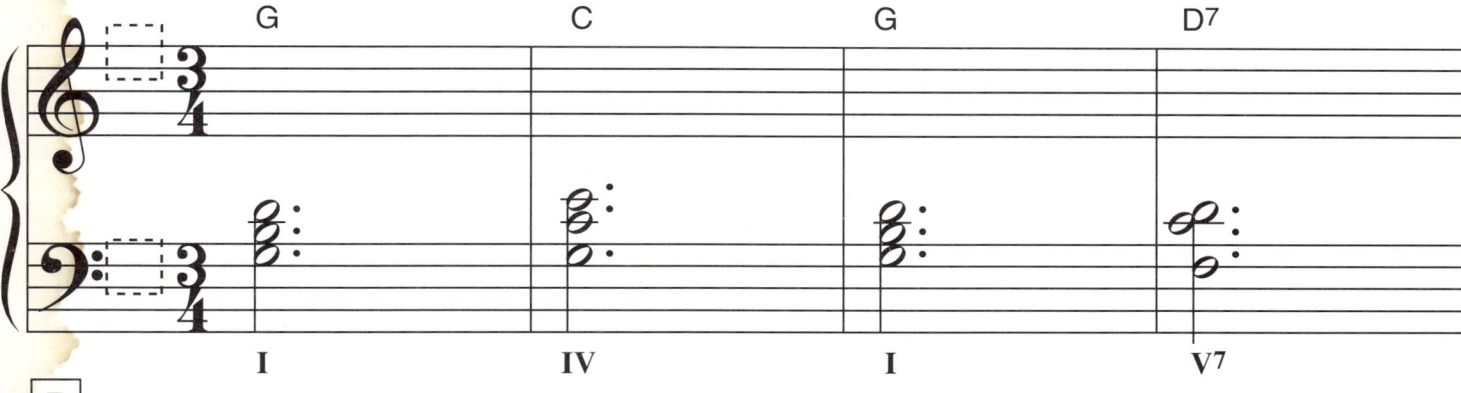

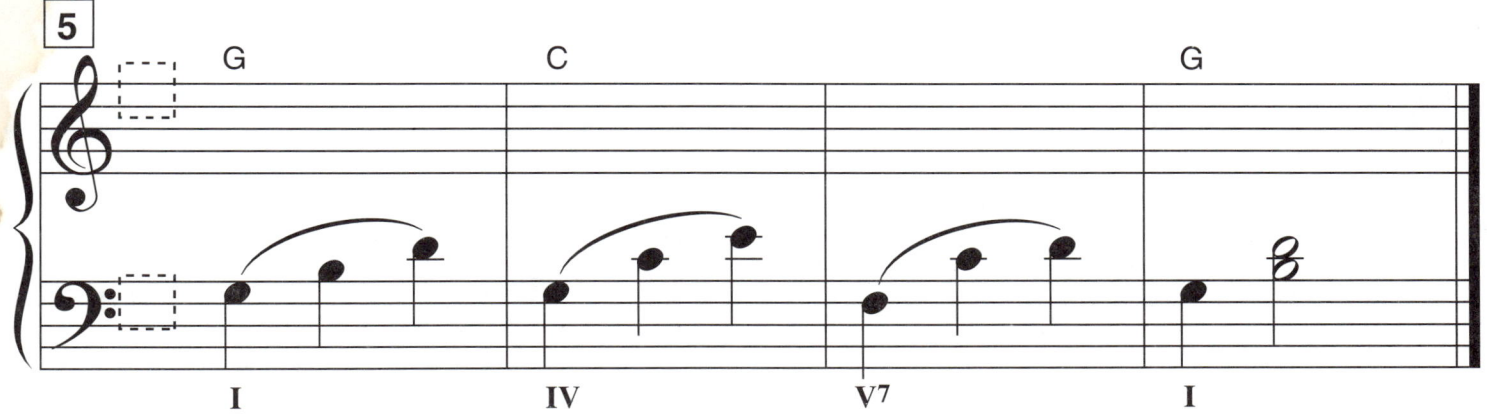

Clap Rap

1. The counting is given at the beginning of *D Major Scale*. Complete the counting (writing 1 & 2 & 3 & 4 &).
2. Clap and say the words to *D Major Scale* with your teacher.
3. Using ♩. ♩ ♫ ♩ and ♪, write the matching rhythm on the lines below the words. Watch for the rhythm ♪♪ ♩ and ♪♪ ♩. (The ties will give you a hint.)
4. Using the D MAJOR SCALE, improvise a melody that matches the rhythm of *D Major Scale*.

Ascending D Major Scale

LH 5   4   3   2   1   3   2   1

Descending D Major Scale

RH 5   4   3   2   1   3   2   1

D Major Scale

4/4 You need | F-sharp, you need C-sharp for the | D Maj-or Scale, Re-

— — — | — — — — — — — | — — — — — —

4   &   1   &   2   &

mem-ber these two sharps and you will | play with-out fail. So

play-ing scales is eas-y if you | take my ad-vice: Put two

tet-ra-chords to-geth-er, you won't | have to think twice!

Broken Chords in D Major

ABA FORM

1. Write an "A" inside the circle at the beginning of the first section of *Mellow-D*. Write a "B" inside the circle at the beginning of the second section (measure 9) indicating a contrasting section of music.

2. **Ⓐ** In **Section A:** Play and count the melody of *Mellow-D* several times. Harmonize *Mellow-D* using BROKEN PRIMARY CHORDS in D MAJOR. Experiment with each chord in every measure. Write the appropriate CHORD SYMBOLS (**I**, **IV** and **V⁷**) in the boxes below each measure.

3. **Ⓑ** In **Section B:** Play the BROKEN PRIMARY CHORDS given in the LH. Using notes from the D MAJOR SCALE, compose an eight measure melody that blends well with the LH. Write the appropriate CHORD SYMBOLS (**I**, **IV** and **V⁷**) in the boxes below each measure.

4. Choose DYNAMIC SIGNS and write *ff*, *f*, *mf*, *mp*, or *pp* in the appropriate places. You may also add *crescendos, diminuendos* and accents.

5. Use the appropriate indications for LEGATO (⌒) and STACCATO (˙𝆺 𝅘𝅥).

6. Play your piece!

Mellow-D

OPTIONAL ACTIVITY: TRANSPOSE *Mellow-D* into C Major and G Major.

Teacher's Examples